To

From

Ellie Claire™ Gift & Paper Corp.
Minneapolis, MN 55438
www.ellieclaire.com

Forever Friends: A Journal
© 2010 by Robin Jones Gunn
www.robingunn.com

ISBN 978-1-935416-82-1

Cover and interior design by Lisa & Jeff Franke

Printed in China

Forever Friends

A JOURNAL

ROBIN JONES GUNN

Ellie Claire™

gift & paper expressions

...inspired by life

"Friendship? Yes, please."

CHARLES DICKENS

My dear, dear friends, if God loved us like this, we certainly ought to love each other.... If we love one another, God dwells deeply within us, and his love becomes complete in us—perfect love!

1 JOHN 4:11-12 MSG

Become friends with God;
he's already a friend with you.

2 Corinthians 5:20 msg

Friendship is a lovely mystery. How is it that two hearts can meet, exchange kindnesses, share smiles and quiet confidences, weather a few rough spots, and somehow end up knit together? Friendship is a gift that grows more valuable with the years. At the beginning, middle, and end of this mysterious gift of friendship is Love. When two friends share not only a genuine love for each other but also an abiding love for God, theirs is truly a Forever Friendship.

At the center of each of our lives we might find that the circle of such Forever Friends is a rather small circle. This makes the gift of their friendship all the richer. Think of how much sweeter your life is because of those few Peculiar Treasures who have come your way and decided to stay.

May your pen take dictation from your heart as you fill these pages with reflections of all the dreams, celebrations, and prayers you share with your Forever Friends.

Warmly,

Robin Jones Gunn

Robin Jones Gunn has written 70 books with over 4 million copies sold worldwide. The first book in the Christy Miller *series released in 1988, and other stories about Christy and her Forever Friends soon followed. Robin and her husband have two grown children and live near Portland, Oregon. To find out more about the Christy Miller novels (and Christy's Forever Friends), please visit www.robingunn.com.*

Section One

Dreaming with My Forever Friends

*God can do anything, you know—far more than you could
ever imagine or guess or request in your wildest dreams!
He does it not by pushing us around but by working within us,
his Spirit deeply and gently within us.*

Ephesians 3:20 MSG

One of my Forever Friends has a unique way of prompting me to dream. Whenever I get discouraged and wistfully toss my dormant wishes into the air, she listens and smiles. I expect the tiny aspirations to fly away and be gone. But she snatches them like fireflies and holds them gently, inviting me to look at the light-giving, airy wonders once more. Then she whispers to my imagination, "Go ahead. Dream. Hope. This is what you were created to do. With God all things are possible."

I look back at all the impossible things in my life that have come to be and I can see that these dreams were God's dreams first. He's the One who plants those tiny possibility thoughts in our hearts. He's the One who brings to pass all that He desires for His children. He created us to hope and dream and wish. Often we stop hoping too soon. We give up when it becomes difficult. And in our lowest moments, we doubt.

How different would your life be if you believed, I mean really believed, that God has extraordinary plans for your life and that He is in the process of fulfilling them right this very minute?

Go ahead. Dream. Hope. Trust God more than you ever have before. Then go whisper those same life-giving words to another discouraged friend and nudge them toward courageous faith when they need it most.

Lord, teach me to be soul-minded. With everything in life may I ask, "What part of this will last for eternity?" Then may I hold on to that part and treasure it in my heart.

RJG

No eye has seen, no ear has heard, and no mind has imagined what God has prepared for those who love him.

1 Corinthians 2:9 NLT

Hope is the thing with feathers—
That perches in the soul—
And sings the tune without the words—
And never stops—at all.

Emily Dickinson

....

....

....

....

....

....

....

....

....

....

....

....

....

....

....

May the God of hope fill you with all joy and peace as you trust in him, so that you may overflow with hope by the power of the Holy Spirit.

ROMANS 15:13 NIV

Whatever your future holds, that future is already held by God.

UNKNOWN

....

....

....

....

....

....

....

....

....

....

....

....

....

....

....

....

....

....

....

....

....

....

....

....

....

....

....

....

....

....

....

....

....

....

....

"*For* I know the plans I have for you," says the Lord. They are plans for good and not for disaster, to give you a future and a hope.

JEREMIAH 29:11 NLT

Every detail of my life goes through the fingers of a loving God who first used those same fingers to form us from the dust of the earth. Lord, I surrender to your deliberate touch.

RJG

O Lord, I will honor and praise your name, for you are my God.
You do such wonderful things! You planned them long ago,
and now you have accomplished them.

Isaiah 25:1 nlt

*G*od shall be my hope, my stay, my guide and lantern to my feet.

SHAKESPEARE

But the eyes of the LORD are on those who fear him,
on those whose hope is in his unfailing love.

PSALM 33:18 NIV

*H*ope is not a granted wish or a favor performed; no, it is far greater than that. It is a zany, unpredictable dependence on a God who loves to surprise us out of our socks.

MAX LUCADO

*C*ommit your way to the LORD; trust in him and he will do this.

When my path is shadowed by darkness, I know, O Lord, that I have run ahead of You. Your guiding light must always be before me, not behind.

RJG

The LORD directs the steps of the godly.
He delights in every detail of their lives.
Though they stumble, they will never fall,
for the LORD holds them by the hand.

Optimism is the faith that leads to achievement. Nothing can be done without hope and confidence.

HELEN KELLER

For you have been my hope, O Sovereign Lord,
my confidence since my youth.

PSALM 71:5 NIV

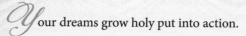

Your dreams grow holy put into action.

ADELAIDE ANN PROCTER

-----

*W*e were like those who dream. Then our mouth was filled with laughter, and our tongue with joyful shouting; Then they said among the nations, "The LORD has done great things for them."

PSALM 126:1-2 NASB

Sometimes to find the key that will unlock the future, we have to see what keys we buried in the past.

RJG

*R*emember the things I have done in the past. For I alone am God! I am God, and there is none like me. Only I can tell you the future before it even happens.

Only dreamers can teach us to soar.

ANNE MARIE PIERCE

This resurrection life you received from God is not a timid, grave-tending life. It's adventurously expectant, greeting God with a childlike "What's next, Papa?"

ROMANS 8:15 MSG

Anger is the fluid love bleeds when you cut it.

C. S. LEWIS

....

....

....

....

....

....

....

....

....

....

....

....

....

....

....

....

....

....

*H*ope deferred makes the heart sick, but a dream fulfilled is a tree of life.

*A*nother note to self: Be bold when the lies come at you.
You belong to Christ, Katie. Follow close after Him.

RJG, *PECULIAR TREASURES*

Pursue a righteous life—a life of wonder, faith, love, steadiness, courtesy. Run hard and fast in the faith. Seize the eternal life, the life you were called to.

1 TIMOTHY 6:11-12 MSG

*L*ift up your eyes. Your heavenly Father waits to bless you—in inconceivable ways to make your life what you never dreamed it could be.

ANNE ORTLUND

I came so they can have real and eternal life, more and better life
than they ever dreamed of.

Piglet sidled up to Pooh.

"Pooh!" he whispered.

"Yes, Piglet?"

"Nothing," said Piglet, taking Pooh's paw. "I just wanted to be sure of you."

A. A. MILNE

The LORD himself goes before you and will be with you; he will never leave you nor forsake you. Do not be afraid; do not be discouraged.

DEUTERONOMY 31:8 NIV

Love is a mystery, it can't be planned. It comes on its own schedule, it's inconvenient and organic, but that's what makes it real. Really good relationships are the ones that come naturally and unforced like waves.

RJG, ELI TO KATIE IN *COMING ATTRACTIONS*

....

....

....

....

....

....

....

....

....

....

....

....

....

....

These three remain: faith, hope and love.
And the greatest of these is love.

1 CORINTHIANS 13:13 NIV

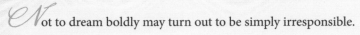ot to dream boldly may turn out to be simply irresponsible.

GEORGE B. LEONARD

Even when there was no reason for hope, Abraham kept hoping.

ROMANS 4:18 NLT

A smile tiptoed onto Christy's lips. She felt a peculiar happiness, but she wasn't sure why. All she knew was that deep inside, the forever part of her heart was still very much alive.

RJG, *Sweet Dreams*

Dear friend, do what I tell you; treasure my careful instructions.
Do what I say and you'll live well.

*Y*ou can never out-give God. I can't wait to see what God's going to give you!

RJG, KATIE TO CHRISTY IN *SWEET DREAMS*

_____

_____

_____

_____

_____

_____

_____

_____

_____

_____

_____

_____

_____

_____

_____

_____

*I*t is clear to us, friends, that God not only loves you very much but also has put his hand on you for something special.

1 THESSALONIANS 1:4 MSG

A true friend will tell you what you need to hear, even when what she or he has to say may not be what you want to hear.

RJG, *TRUE FRIENDS*

Giving an honest answer is a sign of true friendship.

PROVERBS 24:26 CEV

We all mold one another's dreams. We all hold each other's fragile hopes in our hands. We all touch others' hearts.

UNKNOWN

*N*ever let loyalty and kindness leave you!...
Write them deep within your heart.

PROVERBS 3:3 NLT

*G*ood feelings don't always come in the same envelope as the right answer.

RJG, *Peculiar Treasures*

*Y*ou will keep your friends if you forgive them, but you will lose your friends if you keep talking about what they did wrong.

PROVERBS 17:9 CEV

*L*ife is nothing without friendship.

CICERO

This is my command: Love one another the way I loved you. This is the very best way to love. Put your life on the line for your friends.

JOHN 15:13 MSG

*T*hat's just the way God is. He's always on time, but rarely early.

RJG

....
....
....
....
....
....
....
....
....
....
....
....
....
....
....
....
....
....
....
....
....
....

Our Father in heaven, may your name be kept holy. May your Kingdom
come soon. May your will be done on earth, as it is in heaven.

MATTHEW 6:910 NLT

Dream a dream big enough to make God look really good when that dream comes true.

RJG

....

....

....

....

....

....

....

....

....

....

....

....

....

....

....

....

....

*H*umanly speaking, it is impossible. But not with God.
Everything is possible with God.

MARK 10:27 NLT

SECTION TWO

Celebrating My

Forever Friends

And let us not neglect our meeting together,
as some people do, but encourage one another, especially
now that the day of his return is drawing near.

HEBREWS 10:25 NLT

Did you know that in the Old Testament God didn't just suggest that His people set aside time for feasting and celebrating; He commanded it! Friends and family gathered together, sometimes for a day, sometimes for a weeks, and in their celebrating they remembered the goodness and faithfulness of the Lord.

There's a beautiful picture in the book of Nehemiah of what it looked like when a group of friends gathered to read God's Word and was given direction on how to celebrate together.

"Go and celebrate with a feast of rich foods and sweet drinks, and share gifts of food with people who have nothing prepared. This is a sacred day before our Lord. Don't be dejected and sad, for the joy of the LORD is your strength!" (Nehemiah 8:8–10 NIV)

While I was growing up in southern California my friends and I set aside time on summer nights to gather at the beach around the campfire. We would sing, laugh, pray and talk for long hours under the stars. Sometimes we'd be open and honest and share what was going on in our lives. Other times someone would bring a guitar and we'd spend the time singing and reminding each other of all the great things God was doing. A few times we got together just to roast marshmallows and tease each other.

Where do you gather with your friends? How do you naturally encourage and remind each other of all the ways God has been good to you? You can start a new tradition any time you like and be the one to initiate the gathering. So go ahead and celebrate! These pages stand ready to capture your thoughts and memories of good times with good friends.

You're in my heart. You're my friend. I honestly don't know where we go from here, but I'm not worried. God knows. All I know is we're going to spend eternity together with Him. This bracelet is my way of saying, "Here's my friendship. I promise it to you. It's yours forever."

RJG, TODD TO CHRISTY IN *YOURS FOREVER*

....

....

....

....

....

....

....

....

....

....

....

....

....

....

....

....

....
....
....
....
....
....
....
....
....
....
....
....
....
....
....
....
....
....
....

Dear friends, let us love one another, for love comes from God.
Everyone who loves has been born of God and knows God.

1 JOHN 4:7 NIV

Thank you for being a friend.

ANDREW GOLD

....

....

....

....

....

....

....

....

....

....

....

....

....

....

....

....

....

*F*riends come and friends go, but a true friend
sticks by you like family.

PROVERBS 18:24 MSG

If you want to go fast, go alone. If you want to go far, go together.

RJG, AFRICAN PROVERB QUOTED BY ELI TO KATIE
IN *COMING ATTRACTIONS*

....

....

....

....

....

....

....

....

....

....

....

....

....

....

....

....

....

....

Let the peace of Christ keep you in tune with each other,
in step with each other.

COLOSSIANS 3:15 MSG

You can give without loving but you cannot love without giving.

AMY CARMICHAEL

*D*on't look out only for your own interests,
but take an interest in others, too.

Be patient. Be kind. Be faithful. The Lord encompasses the full circle of your life.

RJG

*I*ve loved you the way my Father has loved me.
Make yourselves at home in my love.

If there ever comes a day we can't be together, keep me in your heart. I'll stay there forever.

A. A. MILNE

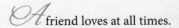

A friend loves at all times.

PROVERBS 17:17 NIV

"*Do* you know what, Kilikina?" Todd caught her tear with his finger and then pressed his finger to his chest directly over his heart. "This is where I save all your tears. Right here, where I hold you in my heart."

RJG, Todd to Christy in *Until Tomorrow*

*I*t is right for me to feel this way about all of you,
since I have you in my heart.

PHILIPPIANS 1:7 NIV

We're the only Bible some people may ever read, so we're like walking, living, breathing Bibles.

RJG, SIERRA IN *NOW PICTURE THIS*

You're here to be light, bringing out the God-colors in the world. God is not a secret to be kept...be generous with your lives. By opening up to others, you'll prompt people to open up with God, this generous Father in heaven.

MATTHEW 5:14,16 MSG

*O*nly people with soft hearts say they are sorry. Soft hearts are the only hearts that God can hold in His hands and mold.

RJG, TODD TO CHRISTY IN *A HEART FULL OF HOPE*

....

....

....

....

....

....

....

....

....

....

....

....

....

....

Jonathan said, "Go in peace! The two of us have vowed friendship in GOD's name, saying, 'GOD will be the bond between me and you, and between my children and your children forever!'"

1 SAMUEL 20:42 MSG

I'm not going anywhere. I'm right here. And I'm staying here. I'm trusting God that He will make our paths straight. He'll show us the next step to take at the right time. All we have to do is keep on being God-Lovers.

RJG, TODD TO CHRISTY IN *AS YOU WISH*

Dear friend, take my advice; it will add years to your life.... I don't want you ending up in blind alleys, or wasting time making wrong turns.... Keep vigilant watch over your heart; that's where life starts.

PROVERBS 4:10, 12, 23 MSG

*Y*ou let God do His God-things in your life and I'll invite God to do His God-things in my life, and we won't compare ourselves with each other. Okay?

RJG, KATIE TO CHRISTY IN *AS YOU WISH*

I want you woven into a tapestry of love, in touch with everything there is to know of God. Then you will have minds confident and at rest, focused on Christ, God's great mystery.

COLOSSIANS 2:2 MSG

A true friend inspires you to believe God has loving plans for you, encourages you to keep pursuing your deepest dreams, and most wonderful of all, celebrates your successes as if they were her own!

UNKNOWN

Everyone will share the story of your wonderful goodness;
they will sing with joy about your righteousness.

PSALM 145:7 NLT

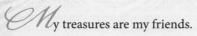

My treasures are my friends.

CONSTANTINE

....
....
....
....
....
....
....
....
....
....
....
....
....
....
....
....
....
....
....
....
....
....
....

I will give you treasures hidden in the darkness—secret riches.
I will do this so you may know that I am the LORD, the God of Israel,
the one who calls you by name.

ISAIAH 45:3 NLT

Is any pleasure on earth as great as a circle of Christian friends by a fire?

C. S. LEWIS

Draw near to God and He will draw near to you.

JAMES 4:8 NASB

*F*riends come and go but true forever friends are never far away from the secret corner of your heart.

RJG, *CHRISTY'S DIARY*

*Y*ou are precious to me. You are honored, and I love you.

A good friend will sharpen your character, draw your soul into the light, and challenge your heart to love in a greater way.

UNKNOWN

But if from there you seek the LORD your God, you will find him if you look for him with all your heart and with all your soul.

DEUTERONOMY 4:29 NIV

With tears in his eyes, Todd said in a hoarse voice, "I'm keeping this." He lifted his hand to reveal the "Forever" bracelet looped between his fingers. "If God ever brings us together again in this world. I'm putting this back on your wrist, and that time, my Kilikina, it will stay on forever."

RJG, TODD TO CHRISTY IN *SWEET DREAMS*

Give thanks to the LORD, for he is good; his love endures forever.

$\mathcal{E}$xperience God in the breathless wonder and startling beauty that is all around you. His sun shines warm upon your face. His wind whispers in the treetops.

WENDY MOORE

....

....

....

....

....

....

....

....

....

....

....

....

....

....

....

....

....

....

He is your praise; he is your God, who performed for you those great
and awesome wonders you saw with your own eyes.

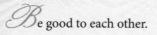

Be good to each other.

GERTRUDE CLAWSON (RJG'S GRANDMA)

....
....
....
....
....
....
....
....
....
....
....
....
....
....
....
....
....
....
....

*W*hat good is it, dear brothers and sisters, if you say you have faith
but don't show it by your actions?

Just pay attention to what God is doing, Katie. That's all I'm saying.
Just pay attention and respond appropriately.

RJG, JULIA TO KATIE IN *COMING ATTRACTIONS*

*Y*ou also must obey the LORD—you must worship him with all your heart and remember the great things he has done for you.

1 SAMUEL 12:24 CEV

Red rover, red rover, send my true friends right over.

UNKNOWN

....

....

....

....

....

....

....

....

....

....

....

....

....

....

....

....

....

....

....

....

....

....

....

....

....

....

....

....

....

....

....

....

....

....

....

I've singled you out, called you by name,
and given you this privileged work.

ISAIAH 45:5 MSG

If we spend all of today thinking about tomorrow, today will be gone, and we will have missed it.

RJG, TODD TO CHRISTY IN *SEVENTEEN WISHES*

*D*o not be afraid, for I have ransomed you.
I have called you by name; you are mine.

ISAIAH 43:1 NLT

When you radiate the love of the Lord, those closest to you can't help but feel the warmth.

RJG

....

....

....

....

....

....

....

....

....

....

....

....

....

....

....

....

....

....

....

Now you've got my feet on the life path, all radiant from the shining of your face. Ever since you took my hand, I'm on the right way.

PSALM 16:11 MSG

I feel I am more blessed than many people because I have this kind of friend in my life. A friend who is always there for me no matter what. A friend who accepts me as I am but loves me too much to let me stay that way. Yes, I would say I am blessed because I have a true friend.

RJG, KATIE IN *TRUE FRIENDS*

....

....

....

....

....

....

....

....

....

....

....

....

....

....

....

....

....

....

....

....

....

....

....

Treat wisdom as a sister, and make understanding your closest friend.

PROVERBS 7:4 NCV

*L*ove is God's greatest gift and His most cherished reward. It is the echo of His own heart, sounded back to Him by us, His children, so that a decaying world might see firsthand the power of resurrection and new life.

RJG, *As You Wish*

....

....

....

....

....

....

....

....

....

....

....

....

....

....

....

....

....

*B*ut I will sing about your strength, my God, and I will celebrate because of your love. You are my fortress, my place of protection in times of trouble.

PSALM 59:16 CEV

SECTION THREE

Praying for My
Forever Friends

I am praying not only for these disciples but also for all
who will ever believe in me through their message.
I pray that they will all be one, just as you and I are one—
as you are in me, Father, and I am in you.

JOHN 17:20 NLT

Do you get a sense of holy awe when you read that Jesus prayed for *us*? I sure do. He prayed for our unity. He prayed that we would be knit together at the heart with each other and with Almighty God.

So, now we have to ask ourselves, what do we pray about when we pray for ourselves and for each other?

During the time my husband and I worked together in youth ministry, one young woman stood out because of the prayer she wrote in her journal during summer camp before her senior year of high school. Her name was Heather. She was feathery, timid, and tenderly concerned about her friends. At the top of one of the pages in her journal she wrote: "My Hit List." On that page she wrote the names of seven friends who were not yet Christians. Then she prayed a simple prayer asking the Lord to go after these friends during their senior year and draw them to Himself. By graduation three of the seven had come to know Christ.

And all timid Heather had done was pray for her friends.

What about you? Which friends would you put on your "Hit List"? The beautiful thing about prayer is that God is available 24/7. You can start praying for those friends right now and be confident that God will hear you.

Pray when you feel like praying. Pray when you don't feel like praying. Pray until you do feel like praying.

UNKNOWN

....

....

....

....

....

....

....

....

....

....

....

....

....

....

....

*C*all to me and I will answer you and tell you great and
unsearchable things you do not know.

JEREMIAH 33:3 NIV

"*Lord* Jesus," Christy whispered, "I want You to hold the key. I want You to decide what should happen in my heart's garden. I'll wait for you."

RJG, CHRISTY MILLER IN *A PROMISE IS FOREVER*

*D*elight yourself in the LORD and he will give you
the desires of your heart.

PSALM 37:4 NIV

Friends warm you with their presence, trust you with their secrets and remember you in their prayers.

UNKNOWN

*M*ay God our Father and the Lord Jesus Christ
give you grace and peace.

If the devil comes knocking on a door you closed long ago,
just call out, "Jesus! It's for you!"

RJG, JULIA TO KATIE IN *ON A WHIM*

So humble yourselves before God. Resist the devil,
and he will flee from you.

JAMES 4:7 NLT

*J*ust slipping into the presence of God can be so exotic and fresh that it delights us enormously.

RICHARD J. FOSTER

*L*isten to my cry for help, my King and my God,
for I pray to no one but you.

$\mathscr{I}$ call it "Hot on His Heels" theology. That's what I think it's like with God. If you want to know what He has to say, you just follow Him. You stay close. You ask and keep asking and you listen. He'll make it clear. The closer you are to Him, the easier it is to hear what He's saying.

RJG, Julia to Katie in *Peculiar Treasures*

....

....

....

....

....

....

....

....

....

....

....

....

....

....

....

....

....

....

....

....

....

....

....

....

....

....

....

....

....

I've prayed for you in particular that you not give in or give out.
When you have come through the time of testing, turn to your
companions and give them a fresh start.

LUKE 22:32 MSG

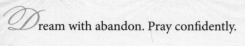

*D*ream with abandon. Pray confidently.

BARBARA JOHNSON

....

....

....

....

....

....

....

....

....

....

....

....

....

....

....

....

....

....

Always be joyful. Never stop praying. Be thankful in all circumstances, for this is God's will for you who belong to Christ Jesus.

1 THESSALONIANS 5:16–18 NLT

$\mathcal{L}$ike art, like music, like so many other disciplines, prayer can only be appreciated when you actually spend time in it. Spending time with the Master will elevate your thinking. The more you pray, the more will be revealed. You will appreciate not only the greatness of prayer, but the greatness of God.

JONI EARECKSON TADA

By day the LORD directs his love, at night his song
is with me—a prayer to the God of my life.

PSALM 42:8 NIV

Then this is where I want to be. Right beside you, forever counting stars.

RJG, CHRISTY TO TODD IN *STARRY NIGHT*

And nd may the Lord make your love for one another and for all people grow and overflow, just as our love for you overflows.

1 Thessalonians 3:12 nlt

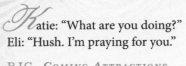

Katie: "What are you doing?"
Eli: "Hush. I'm praying for you."

RJG, *Coming Attractions*

....

....

....

....

....

....

....

....

....

....

....

....

....

....

....

....

....

....

....

Every time I think of you, I give thanks to my God. Whenever I pray,
I make my requests for all of you with joy.

PHILIPPIANS 1:3–4 NLT

I thank God, my friend, for the blessing you are...for the joy of your laughter...the comfort of your prayers...the warmth of your smile.

UNKNOWN

When I am hurting, I find comfort in your promise that leads to life.

PSALM 119:50 CEV

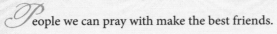

$\mathcal{P}$eople we can pray with make the best friends.

JANETTE OKE

....

....

....

....

....

....

....

....

....

....

....

....

....

....

....

....

....

....

....

....

*O*h, that I might have my request,
that God would grant what I hope for.

JOB 6:8 NIV

We are silent at the beginning of the day because God should have the first word, and we are silent before going to sleep because the last word also belongs to God.

Dietrich Bonhoeffer

....
....
....
....
....
....
....
....
....
....
....
....
....
....
....
....
....
....
....
....
....
....
....
....
....
....

Morning, noon, and night you hear my concerns and my complaints.

PSALM 55:17 CEV

I guess I can't change anything. Only God can. I can ask Him to do something supernatural in a natural way.

RJG, CHRISTY IN *A TIME TO CHERISH*

*D*on't worry about anything; instead, pray about everything. Tell God what you need, and thank him for all he has done. Then you will experience God's peace, which exceeds anything we can understand. His peace will guard your hearts and minds as you live in Christ Jesus.

PHILIPPIANS 4:6–7 NLT

A joyful heart is like the sunshine of God's love, the hope of eternal happiness, a burning flame of God.... And if we pray, we will become that sunshine of God's love—in our own home, the place where we live, and in the world at large.

MOTHER TERESA

Then Christ will make his home in your hearts as you trust in him.
Your roots will grow down into God's love and keep you strong.

When seeds of kindness are sown prayerfully in the garden plot of our lives, we may be sure that there will be a bountiful harvest of blessing for both us and others.

W. PHILLIP KELLER

....
....
....
....
....
....
....
....
....
....
....
....
....
....
....
....
....
....

Sow righteousness, reap love. It's time to till the ready earth, it's time to dig in with God.

HOSEA 10:12 MSG

To live in prayer together is to walk in love together.

MARGARET JACOBS

....

....

....

....

....

....

....

....

....

....

....

....

....

....

....

....

....

....

....

....

....

....

O Lord,...listen to the prayers of those of us
who delight in honoring you.

This morning I padded outside just as the sun was rising. My bare feet left tender prints in the dew-laced grass. A single bird perched at the very top of the shivering birch tree and sang out a call to worship. I lifted my face to the heavens to pray. For one piercing moment I felt my kinship to Eve and the immediacy she had with You in that first garden. You were so close, Lord.

RJG

....

....

....

....

....

....

....

....

....

....

....

....

....

....

Seek God while he's here to be found,
pray to him while he's close at hand.

*Y*our prayers move God to change the world. You may not understand the mystery of prayer. You don't need to. But this much is clear: Actions in heaven begin when someone prays on earth. What an amazing thought!

MAX LUCADO

Then he said, "Don't be afraid, Daniel. Since the first day you began to pray for understanding and to humble yourself before your God, your request has been heard in heaven. I have come in answer to your prayer."

We must begin to believe that God, in the mystery of prayer, has entrusted us with a force that can move the Heavenly world, and can bring its power down to earth.

ANDREW MURRAY

....

....

....

....

....

....

....

....

....

....

....

....

....

....

....

....

....

....

I also pray that you will understand the incredible greatness of God's power for us who believe him.

Seven days without prayer makes one weak.

ALLEN E. VARTLETT

---

*W*e also pray that you will be strengthened with all his glorious power so you will have all the endurance and patience you need. May you be filled with joy, always thanking the Father.

COLOSSIANS 1:11-12 NLT

Dear Future Husband, I was thinking today about friends and about how I want us to always be good friends—before and after we're married.... I just wanted you to know that I'm praying for you and thinking about you. Your friend, Christy.

RJG, CHRISTY MILLER IN *TRUE FRIENDS*

So we have not stopped praying for you since we first heard about you.
We ask God to give you complete knowledge of his will and to give you
spiritual wisdom and understanding.

COLOSSIANS 1:9 NLT

*G*od's greatest concern is not the length of our prayers, nor the correctness of our language, but the attitude of our hearts.

LEIGHTON FORD

....

....

....

....

....

....

....

....

....

....

....

....

....

....

....

....

....

Create in me a clean heart, O God, and renew a steadfast spirit within me.

PSALM 51:10 NASB

$\mathcal{D}$o you know why the mighty God of the universe chooses to answer prayer? It is because His children ask. God delights in our asking. He is pleased at our asking. His heart is warmed by our asking.

RICHARD J. FOSTER

If you remain in me and my words remain in you,
ask whatever you wish, and it will be given you.

JOHN 15:7 NIV

The LORD bless you and keep you; the LORD make his face shine upon you and be gracious to you; the LORD turn his face toward you and give you peace.

NUMBERS 6:24–26 NIV